The Big Book of Giant Dinosaurs

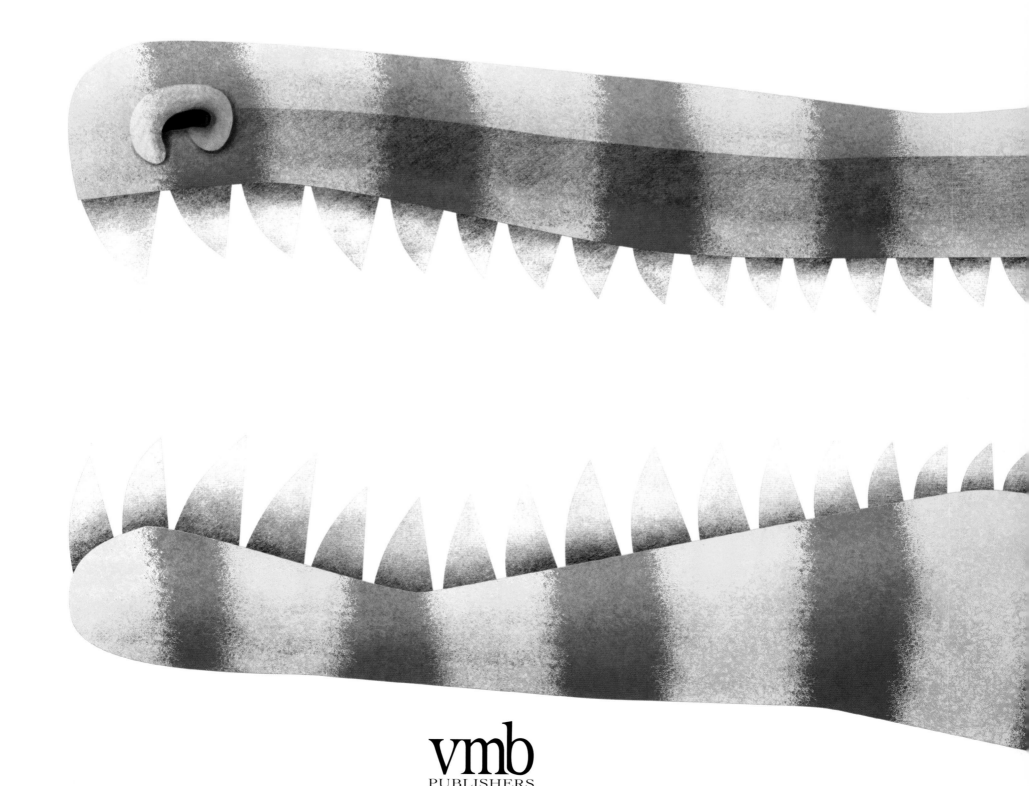

vmb
PUBLISHERS

Introduction

Everything we know about dinosaurs today is due to the discovery of their **petrified bones**, which have become **fossils**. By studying their skeletons, paleontologists are able to tell us, first of all, that dinosaurs were numerous and that they were **very different from each other**.

Paleontologists are able to make many hypotheses about what dinosaurs did in their daily life such as, for example, what they ate, how they walked, how they attacked their prey, or how they defended themselves from their enemies. Unfortunately, some characteristics of dinosaurs are still missing: the color of their skin, for example, or the color of their eyes remain unknown, as there is no trace of these in the fossils. It is likely, however, that the colors of their skin and feathers were much more varied than was previously thought. What we do know for sure is that some of these ancient reptiles were the largest animals that ever lived on Earth; they were so large that we cannot even get an exact idea of their size!

The Brontosaurus was an **enormous** dinosaur and moved on land by walking on **four legs** that were thick and giant. We can only imagine how loud its footsteps would have been! As heavy as **four elephants**, it made the earth tremble when it walked! Its tail was long and flexible, becoming thinner at the end, and was probably used as a **whip** in case of attack by its enemies.

It lived during the Jurassic period, 150 million years ago.

It was 72.2 feet (22 m) long and fed on vegetables.

Brontosaurus

This dinosaur had front legs equipped with **incredibly large claws** – the longest in the animal kingdom **from the past and even today** – that were similar to swords and potentially very deadly. Despite this, the Therizinosaurus was actually a **peaceful animal,** using its claws only to **collect the twigs** that it fed on.

It lived during the Cretaceous period, 70 million years ago.

It was 32.8 feet (10 m) long and fed on vegetables.

Therizinosaurus

The Spinosaurus's most visible characteristic was the row of **spines on its back**, which supported a **sail made of skin**. This dinosaur loved to stay **long hours in the water**, where it could find its favorite food, **fish**, catching it mostly by using its mouth, which was equipped with an **elongated snout**, similar to that of the crocodile.

It lived during the Cretaceous period, 100 million years ago,
ate fish, and was 49.2 feet (15 m) long.

Spinosaurus

The Tyrannosaurus rex is perhaps the **most famous** dinosaur for its size and appearance, which make it absolutely **terrifying even after millions of years!** Its large mouth was armed with **long teeth**: wide open, it was large enough to capture prey as large as a Triceratops. Its front legs had only **two clawed fingers** and were so short that they were practically useless. Its hind legs, instead, were large and muscular, perfect for **running fast**, although only for short distances.

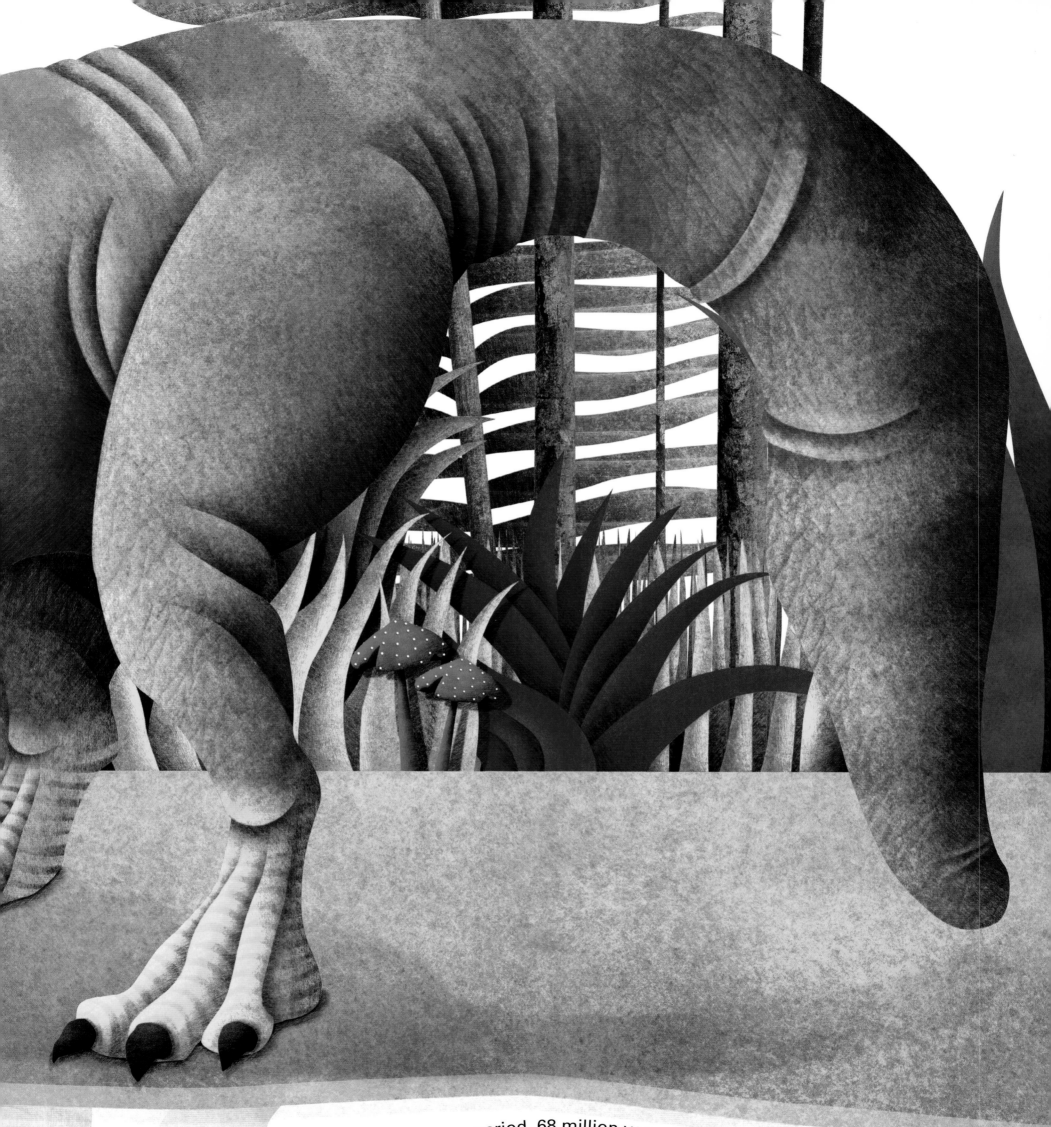

It lived during the Cretaceous period, 68 million years ago.
It was 41 feet (12.5 m) long and was a carnivore.

Tyrannosaurus rex

The Carnotaurus was lighter than the T. rex, but just as **ferocious**. Like its famous counterpart, the Carnotaurus had **short arms** that were **practically useless**, and **strong hind legs** that allowed it to **run fast**. On its head, right above its eyes, it was equipped with **two small horns**: researchers do not know what they were for, perhaps to **protect its head** during fights between the males of its species.

It lived in the Cretaceous period, 70 million years ago.

It was 29.5 feet (9 m) long and was a carnivore.

Carnotaurus

Try to imagine large herds of dinosaurs that moved together even for long journeys, looking for plants to feed on. One of the dinosaurs of this type is the Edmontosaurus, a large, peaceful dinosaur, as heavy as two rhinoceroses and as long as four cars in a row. It walked on land, collecting large quantities of hard plants with its flattened duck beak, which it then grinded up finely using numerous teeth arranged in several rows.

It was 49.2 feet (15 m) long, lived during the Cretaceous period, 70 million years ago, and was herbivorous.

Edmontosaurus

This herbivorous dinosaur was **peaceful**... at least until it was attacked: when it was threatened, it **knew how to defend itself well!** Its **enormous head** was armed with **three horns:** two above its eyes that were as long as a man's arm, and a shorter one on its snout. Behind its head, a large **bone collar** protected its neck and part of its back **like a shield.** The animal was only vulnerable from behind and that's why the Triceratops **lived in herds,** protecting each other. **Baby dinosaurs,** in particular, were kept safe at the **center of the group.**

It lived during the Cretaceous period, 65 million years ago, fed on a diet of vegetables, and was 29.5 feet (9 m) long.

Triceratops

Iguanodons were large herbivorous dinosaurs which **walked on their hind legs**
resting on their toes, preferring to keep their front legs free to gather plants to feed on, bringing
food up to their beak. Their **thumb** was equipped with a **robust claw**, perhaps used
to **break the shells** of fruit, or as a defense mechanism from predators
and in fights with dinosaurs of the same species.

It was 42.7 feet (13 m) long, lived during the Cretaceous period,

125 million years ago, and was an herbivore.

Iguanodon

The Magnapaulia had **a bone crest** on its head, which served above all as a **sound box** to increase the intensity of the sounds produced by its nose. Its back protruded greatly because of the extraordinarily **tall bones of its spine**. It moved in a pack, traveling on very long **migrations** looking for large quantities of leaves to eat.

It lived during the Cretaceous period, 75 million years ago.

It was 49.2 feet (15 m) long and was herbivorous.

Magnapaulia

What is most surprising about this large herbivorous dinosaur is its head, which had
a **tube-shaped bone crest**, inside of which there were **various channels connected to its nose**.
It is thought that the animal inhaled air, to produce a sound like a **trumpet**! The Parasaurolophus lived in **herds**:
in calm situations, it **moved on four legs**, but at the first sign of danger, the whole group fled, preferring to
run two-legged, which ensured greater speed.

It was 31.2 feet (9.5 m) long, lived during the Cretaceous period, 75 million years ago, and was herbivorous.

Parasaurolophus

The Stegosaurus is famous for the **two rows of bone plates along its back,** which made it recognizable at first sight. Paleontologists think that they were used to scare off enemies or to attract partners of the same species. Its real defense weapon was its **tail,** which was **equipped with dangerous spikes**. Its head, small compared to the body, makes researchers think that it was **not a particularly intelligent** animal.

It lived during the Jurassic period, 150 million years ago.

It was 29.5 feet (9 m) long and was herbivorous.

Stegosaurus

This "tank" dinosaur was practically **unassailable** by most predators,
thanks to the **hardy, pointed bone plates** that covered its entire body, including
its head. Even the **tip of its tail** was dangerous because it was armed with a **heavy
club** that it used to **deliver violent blows** to its assailants.

It lived during the Cretaceous period, 70 million years ago.

It was 32.8 feet (10 m) long and was herbivorous.

Ankylosaurus

The Gigantoraptor probably looked more like a **bird** than a reptile. It had a **large toothless beak** and moved on **two legs**. Evidence of its feathers has not yet been found, but researchers imagine that it had them all over its body. As tall as a **giraffe** and almost as heavy as a **hippopotamus**, it ate a bit of everything: plants and fruits, small animals, and eggs.

It was 26.2 feet (8 m) long, lived during the Cretaceous period,
65 million years ago, and was omnivorous.

Gigantoraptor

The Styracosaurus was a relative of the Triceratops, from which
it was distinguished by its **slightly smaller size** and **six long spikes**
distributed along the edge of the bone collar that protected its neck.
The spikes grew with age and baby dinosaurs, which lacked them, relied
on the **proximity of adults** to escape predators.

It lived during the Cretaceous period, 75 million years ago.

It was 18 feet (5.5 m) long and fed on vegetables.

Styracosaurus

What was the **helmet** that the Corythosaurus wore on its head used for?
Researchers still **do not know!** It was a **ridge of bone**, flattened on the sides,
which was connected to its nostrils and may have been used to **produce
sounds**, or simply to improve its sense of smell.
In adult males, the helmet could be up to **3.3 feet (1 m) long**.

It lived during the Cretaceous period, 75 million years ago.

It was 32.8 feet (10 m) long and was herbivorous.

Corythosaurus

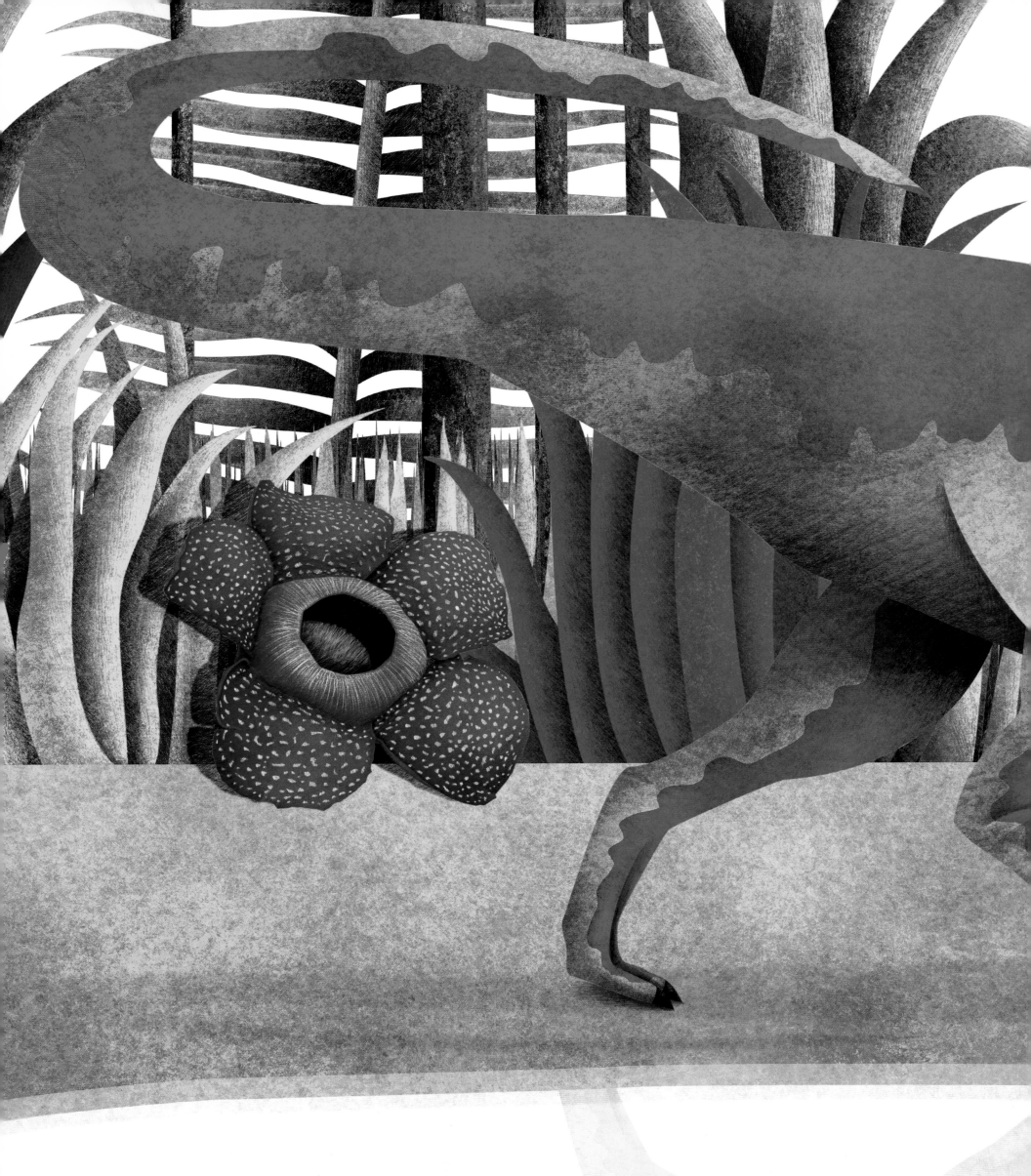

That's a very hard head indeed! The upper part of the skull of the Pachycephalosaurus resembled a **motorcycle helmet of**: it was actually formed by **very hard, thick bones**. Scars found on some remains have led researchers to believe that **the males butted heads,** probably to impress the females, and that the strengthened bones **helped to avoid damage to the brains** of these hardheaded dinosaurs.

It lived during the Cretaceous period, 70 million years ago.

It was 23 feet (7 m) long and was herbivorous.

Pachycephalosaurus

The Deinocheirus's **arms were almost 6.6 feet (2 m) long**, with **three-fingered** hands equipped with **long pointed nails**, which it probably used to collect food. **It was not picky**: it ate everything edible that it found, including fruits, leaves, aquatic plants and even small fish, and it usually **swallowed stones** that helped it to digest the food it had eaten by **moving them around in its stomach**.

It was 36 feet (11 m) long, lived during the Cretaceous period,

70 million years ago, and was omnivorous.

Deinocheirus

Very similar in appearance to the T. rex, but larger, the Giganotosaurus was the undisputed ruler, the super-predator of its environment! It weighed as much as four rhinoceroses, but this did not prevent it from running fast to chase its prey. It may have hunted in packs like wolves, as there was strength in numbers, and multiple dinosaurs could have together taken down prey of enormous dimensions, like the Argentinosaurus.

It lived during the Cretaceous period, 100 million years ago.

It was 42.5 feet (13 m) long and fed on meat.

Giganotosaurus

Francesca Cosanti

Born in Martina Franca (Italy) in 1985, she attended an illustration and multimedia animation course at the European Institute of Design in Rome, and then an illustration course at the Academy of Illustration Officina b5 (Rome) along with various intensive courses with internationally renowned illustrators.

She has worked as an illustrator since 2005 and, at the same time, has taught in various institutions as an expert in illustration and art techniques, graphic design, and multimedia software. In 2007, she won first prize for the Logo of the Italian Presidency of the Council of the Ministers, Department of European Affairs.

She currently works as an illustrator for publishing and advertising companies, associations, and agencies and, in her spare time, dedicates herself to her passions: travel, food, swimming, books, photography and long walks.

In recent years she has illustrated various titles for White Star Kids.

VMB Publishers® is a registered trademark property of White Star s.r.l.

© 2019, 2020 White Star s.r.l.
Piazzale Luigi Cadorna, 6 - 20123 Milan, Italy
www.whitestar.it

Translation: TxTradurre, Rome

ISBN 978-88-540-4424-1
1 2 3 4 5 6   24 23 22 21 20

Printed in Heshan, China

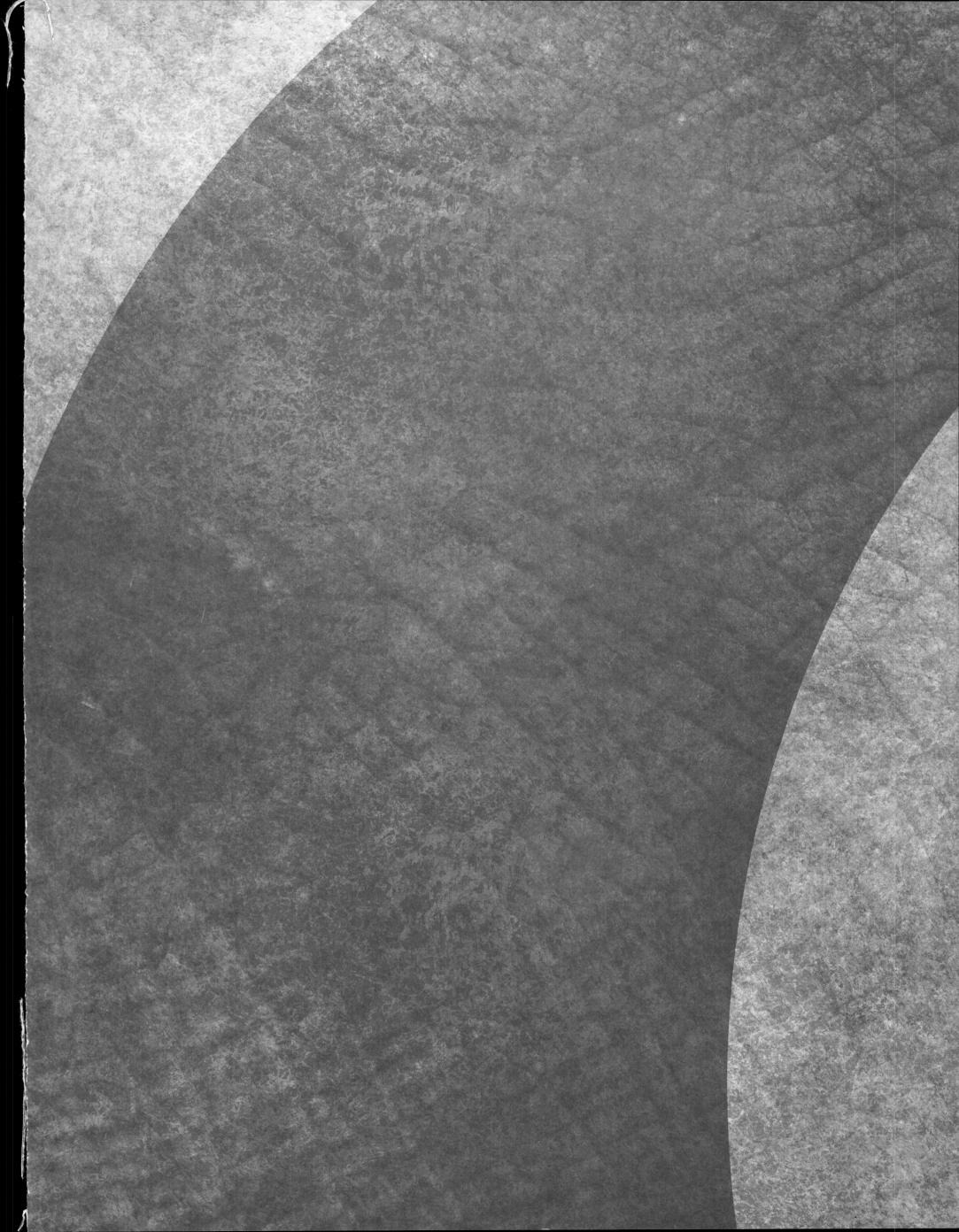

vmb
PUBLISHERS

The Small Book of
Tiny Dinosaurs

Introduction

Do you think that all dinosaurs were huge and scary? Nothing could be more wrong! Next to enormous, terrifying dinosaurs also lived small, sometimes graceful creatures that were the size of a pet or just a little larger. Unlike their extra-large-sized counterparts, however, mini-dinosaurs are not very well-known: because of their reduced size, their skeletons have only been preserved in a few cases and therefore the discovery of their remains is very rare. Moreover, only a few bones are brought to light

and they are broken into such
small fragments that it takes
paleontologists years to study them, in many
cases giving up on rebuilding the possible
appearance of the animal.
Many dinosaurs that you will find in this
book will probably be unknown
to you, but it will be fun to discover
the secrets of their little lives.
There is still so much to understand and
study that, if you become a paleontologist,
you can make your contribution to unraveling
the many mysteries that still surround these
prehistoric animals.

It lived during the Triassic period, 230 million years ago.
It was 5 feet (1.5 m) long and fed on vegetables.

Saturnalia

The Saturnalia was a small dinosaur that lived in the forest and is also one of the oldest dinosaurs found to date. From animals like it, huge dinosaurs like the Brontosaurus and Argentinosaurus evolved, millions of years later: look for them in the other book and you'll see what a difference there was!

Ohmdenosaurus

The Ohmdenosaurus belongs to the Brontosaurus family and, like it, **fed on vegetables**, even if they were much smaller! It is not well-known as a dinosaur as only a **few bones of one paw** have been discovered and these are highly damaged.

It lived during the Jurassic period, 180 million years ago. It was 13 feet (4 m) long and ate vegetables.

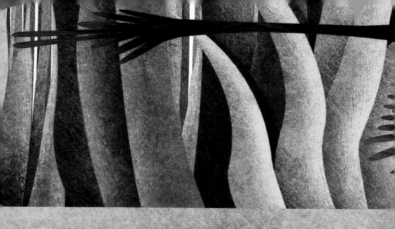

Microraptor

Many dinosaurs **had feathers** and the Microraptor is proof of this fact. In addition to a **long plumed tail**, it had **four wings**: the front ones were long and narrow to support the animal in the air, and the shorter back ones were useful for making quick turns in the thick of the **forest**.

It was 16-32 inches (40-80 cm) long, a carnivore, and lived 125 million years ago, in the Cretaceous period.

This miniature dinosaur had a body covered
with quills and feathers, just like a **small bird**.
On its front leg, the **third finger** was extraordinarily
long and was used by the Scansoriopteryx
to climb trees.

Scansoriopteryx

was only 12 inches (30 cm) long and lived during the Jurassic period, 169 million years ago. It ate insects.

It lived during the Jurassic period, 150 million years ago.

It was 13 feet (4 m) long and was a carnivore.

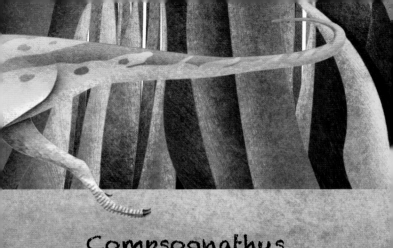

Compsognathus

The Compsognathus walked on its hind legs and its front ones were shorter and **equipped with claws**. It was a **hunter** of small prey, even those as fast as lizards, which it captured thanks to its **agility**: its body was slender and it had a long tail which allowed it to make **lightning-fast jumps**.

Epidexipteryx

Like many small dinosaurs, the Epidexipteryx was also plumed. Its feathers, however, **did not allow it to fly** and it could **only glide**, thanks also to a membrane of skin that stretched between its long fingers. Its tail feathers, on the other hand, similar to long ribbons, were **ornamental**.

It lived during the Jurassic period, ate meat and insects, and was 14-16 inches (35-40 cm) long.

It lived during the Cretaceous period, 120 million years ago.
It was 20 inches (50 cm) long and fed on meat and insects.

Mei long

With a slender body and long legs, the Mei long was
a **racing champion** and a **predator** of small animals,
probably insects, which it identified easily with its **large
eyes**. Like many modern birds, it slept by putting its
head under its shoulder.

Parvicursor

Its **long back legs** allowed it to **run fast**, while the front ones were short and had a **single** functioning **finger**, equipped with a **robust claw**. Paleontologists hypothesize that this claw was used to empty the nests of insects and feed on the **larvae**.

It lived during the Cretaceous period, ate meat and insects, and was 16 inches (40 cm) long.

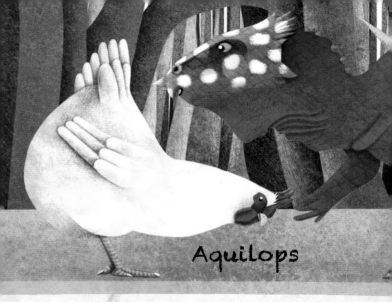

Aquilops

This dinosaur had a very unusual nose: on its **beak**, similar to that of an eagle, there was a **small pointed horn**, which may have been used by the Aquilops to **attract the females** of its species.

It was 2.3 feet (70 cm) long, lived during the Cretaceous period, 109 million years ago, and was herbivorous.

It lived during the Triassic period, 215 million years ago, was 2.5 feet (70 cm) long, and was omnivorous.

Agnosphitys

The few remains of this dinosaur are still a **mystery to science:** researchers know that it is **very ancient,** that it walked on **two legs,** and that it probably ate everything edible that it could capture with its teeth.

It lived during the Cretaceous period, 105 million years ago, and it was 3.3 feet (1 m) long.

.eaellynasaura

Researchers think that the Leaellynasaura lived near the
outh Pole, where, at that time, the temperature was
ot as cold as it is today. It was covered in warm, fluffy
feathers and had a long tail three times the
ngth of its body, which it wrapped around itself
on the coldest days.

Fulgurotherium

It lived near the South Pole, where, millions of years ago, vas forests were home to a **wide variety of animals**. In the cold months, Fulgurotherium dinosaurs may have **migrated to the north** in search of milder temperatures and food. However, researchers also believe that it spent the winter in **burrows dug underground**.

It lived during the Cretaceous period, 130 million years ago.
It was 5 feet (1.5 m) long and fed on vegetables.

It was 2 feet (60 cm) long, lived during the Cretaceous period, 70 million years ago, and was herbivorous.

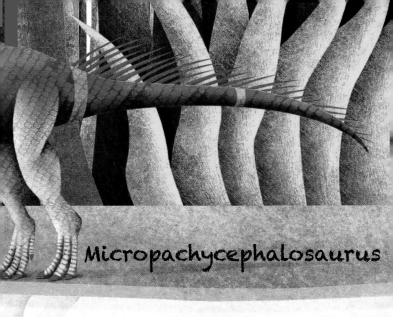

Micropachycephalosaurus

Little is known about this small dinosaur: it was herbivorous, it moved around quickly on two legs, and escaped predators using its great agility. It is likely that it had a beak similar to that of parrots, which it used to shred the hardest leaves.

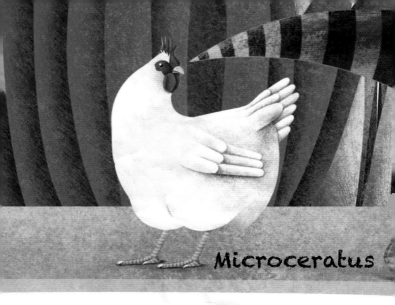

Microceratus

The Microceratus lived in the desert, where it was able to graze on the few hard plants that existed there using its **small, thin, sharp beak**. Although it was rather agile, it was easy prey for carnivorous dinosaurs, from which it escaped by hiding in tunnels that it **dug in the ground**.

It was 2 feet (60 cm) long, lived during the Cretaceous period, 90 million years ago, and fed on vegetables.

It lived during the Cretaceous period, 80 million years ago, it was 20 inches (50 cm) long, and was herbivorous.

Gryphoceratops

The Gryphoceratops looked like an animal out of a book of fairy tales: it had a **beak** similar to that of an eagle, a flashy **collar,** and may have had **small horns**. It lived in the forest, where it spent its days looking for its favorite food: the softest leaves of the trees.

It lived during the Cretaceous period, ate vegetables, and was 2 feet (60 cm) long.

Wannanosaurus

It certainly had a **hard head**! The bones of its skull were actually **very thick** but, given their small size, they were not an effective defense weapon against larger predators. When facing danger, the Wannanosaurus preferred to **escape or hide** in the thick of the forest.

Tatisaurus

Based only on the few remains that have been found, the reconstruction of this dinosaur is still a mystery. It is likely, however, that the Tatisaurus was **partly armored**, with **bony spikes** along its entire body. This made it an **indigestible mouthful** for larger predators.

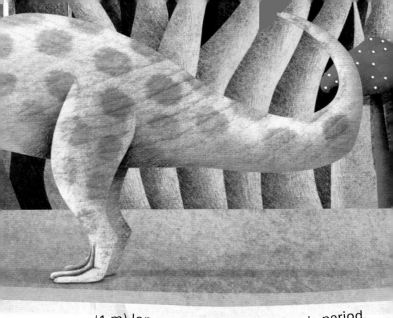

It was 3.3 feet (1 m) long, lived during the Jurassic period, 190 million years ago, and was herbivorous.

It lived during the Jurassic period, 200 million years ago.

It was 4 feet (1.2 m) long and fed on vegetables.

Scutellosaurus

This dinosaur had **small bone shields** along its back and on the sides of its body, which protected it from enemy fangs and claws. It also had a very long tail, which it may have used **as a whip**, but, in case of danger, it is more likely that it preferred to **roll itself into a ball**, like an **armadillo**.

vmb
PUBLISHERS

VMB Publishers® is a registered trademark property of White Star s.r.l.

© 2019, 2020 White Star s.r.l.
Piazzale Luigi Cadorna, 6 - 20123 Milan, Italy
www.whitestar.it

Translation: TxTradurre, Rome

ISBN 978-88-540-4424-1
1 2 3 4 5 6   24 23 22 21 20

Printed in Heshan, China